CORNERSTONES OF FREEDOM™

SECOND SERIES

Tom McGowen

Children's Press®
A Division of Scholastic Inc.
New York • Toronto • London • Auckland • Sydney
Mexico City • New Delhi • Hong Kong
Danbury, Connecticut

Photographs © 2004: AP/Wide World Photos: 19, 24, 31, 32, 39, 44 right; Archives of the YIVO Institute for Jewish Research: 4; Corbis Images: 7, 15, 18, 21, 23 (Bettmann), 14, 16, 38 (Owen Franken), 5, 30 (Hulton-Deutsch Collection), 8, 10, 11, 44 top; Hulton|Archive/Getty Images: cover bottom, 9, 20, 29, 33, 34, 35, 40, 41, 44 bottom, 45 bottom left; Library of Congress: 22, 26; National Archives and Records Administration: 12, 13, 27, 28, 36, 37, 45 bottom right; U.S. Army Photo/Baker: 6; U.S. Navy Photo via SODA: 3, 45 top; U.S. Coast Guard via SODA: cover top.

Library of Congress Cataloging-in-Publication Data

McGowen, Tom.

D-Day / Tom McGowen.

p. cm. — (Cornerstones of freedom. Second series)

[Includes index.]

Summary: Discusses the events leading up to the Allied invasion of Normandy in 1944.

ISBN 0-516-24245-8

1. World War, 1939–1945—Campaigns—France—Normandy—Juvenile literature. 2. Operation Overlord—Juvenile literature. 3. Normandy (France)—History—Juvenile literature. [1. World War, 1939–1945—Campaigns—France—Normandy. 2. Operation Overlord.] I. Title. II. Series.

D756.1.M397 2004

940.54'21421—dc22

2003016941

1 2 3 4 5 6 7 8 9 10 R 13 12 11 10 09 08 07 06 05 04

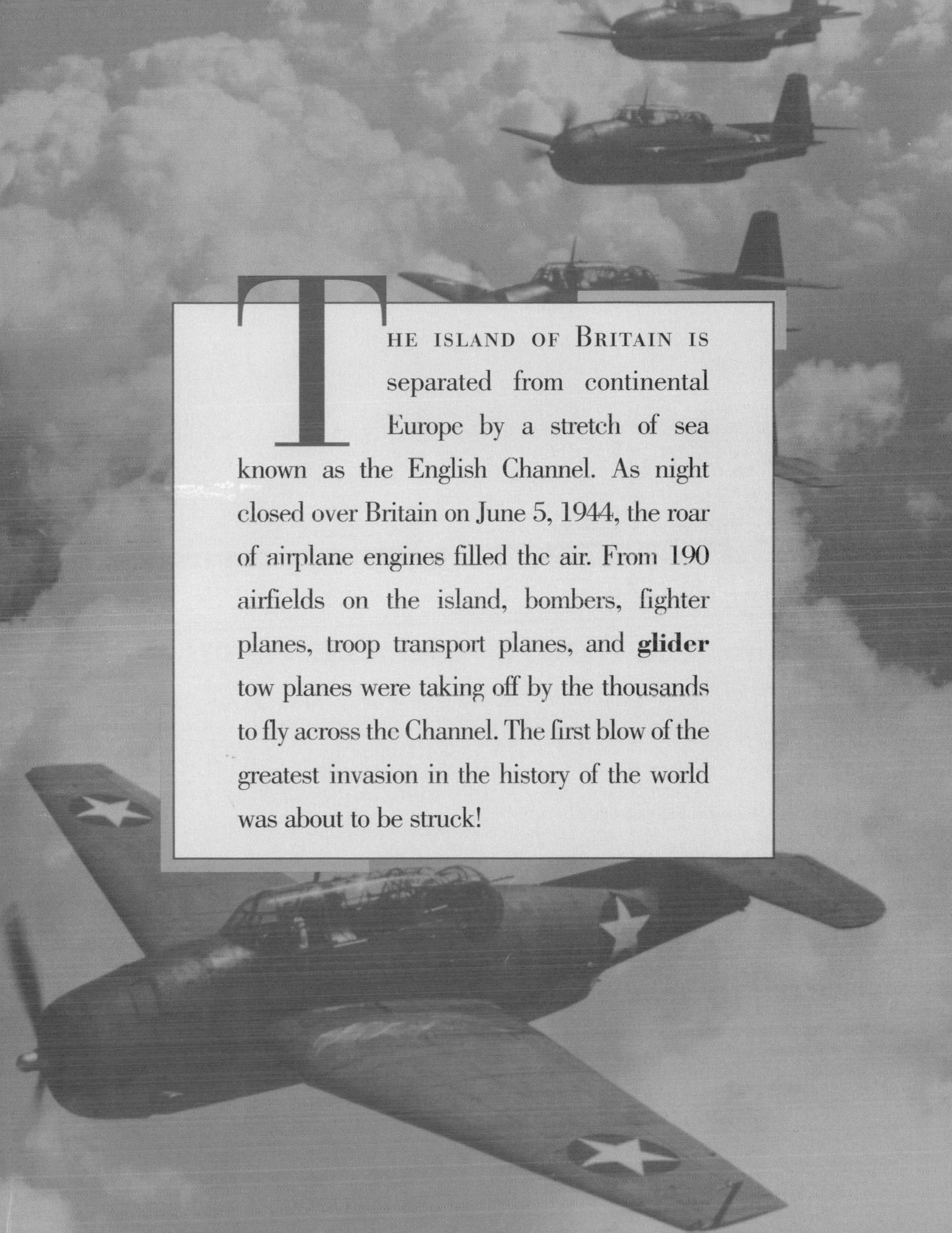

THE ISLAND OF BRITAIN IS separated from continental Europe by a stretch of sea known as the English Channel. As night closed over Britain on June 5, 1944, the roar of airplane engines filled the air. From 190 airfields on the island, bombers, fighter planes, troop transport planes, and **glider** tow planes were taking off by the thousands to fly across the Channel. The first blow of the greatest invasion in the history of the world was about to be struck!

Hitler is enthusiastically welcomed by a crowd of supporters in Germany. Beloved by many Germans, Hitler would lead his country down the path to war.

A WORLD ABLAZE WITH WAR

World War II began on September 1, 1939. The **dictator** of Germany, Adolf Hitler, ordered the German army to invade Poland. Fearing that Hitler intended to conquer all of Europe, if not the whole world, France and Great Britain declared war on Germany.

Poland had been conquered in only forty-seven days. A few months later, German forces conquered Denmark and Norway. Then they struck into Belgium and the Netherlands before pushing into France. France was conquered in only forty-three days.

NAZI GERMANY

From 1933 to 1945, Germany was ruled by a political party called the Nazis (Naht-zees). The Nazi leader was Adolf Hitler, and he had total power. Anyone opposing him was sent to prison or executed. He caused the deaths of millions of people in special prisons called concentration camps, where they were starved, tortured, and murdered.

In 1941 the United States was pulled into the war when Japan, Hitler's **ally**, attacked Hawai'i. Hitler declared war on the United States. The whole world was now ablaze with war.

By 1944, the United States and Great Britain were allies. In Italy, American and British troops battled to push the Nazi soldiers back into Germany. The Americans and British, together with Canadian and French troops, had built up a huge force in Britain. They planned to launch an invasion into Western Europe to push the Germans out of

German cavalry soldiers ride through Paris in 1940 after occupying the city.

the countries they had conquered there. The invasion force would cross the English Channel and strike somewhere on the coast of France, which was occupied by German armies.

German military leaders knew the invasion was coming, but they did not know where it would hit. Field Marshal Gerd von Rundstedt, commander of all German forces in Western Europe, felt the most likely place for the invasion would be the region of France called Pas de Calais. This area is 20 miles (32 kilometers) from the coast of Britain. Most German generals agreed. In fact, German scout planes flying off the coast of England reported a huge buildup of

The U.S. Army's 10th Mountain Division prepares to capture Mt. Belvedere in northern Italy from German troops.

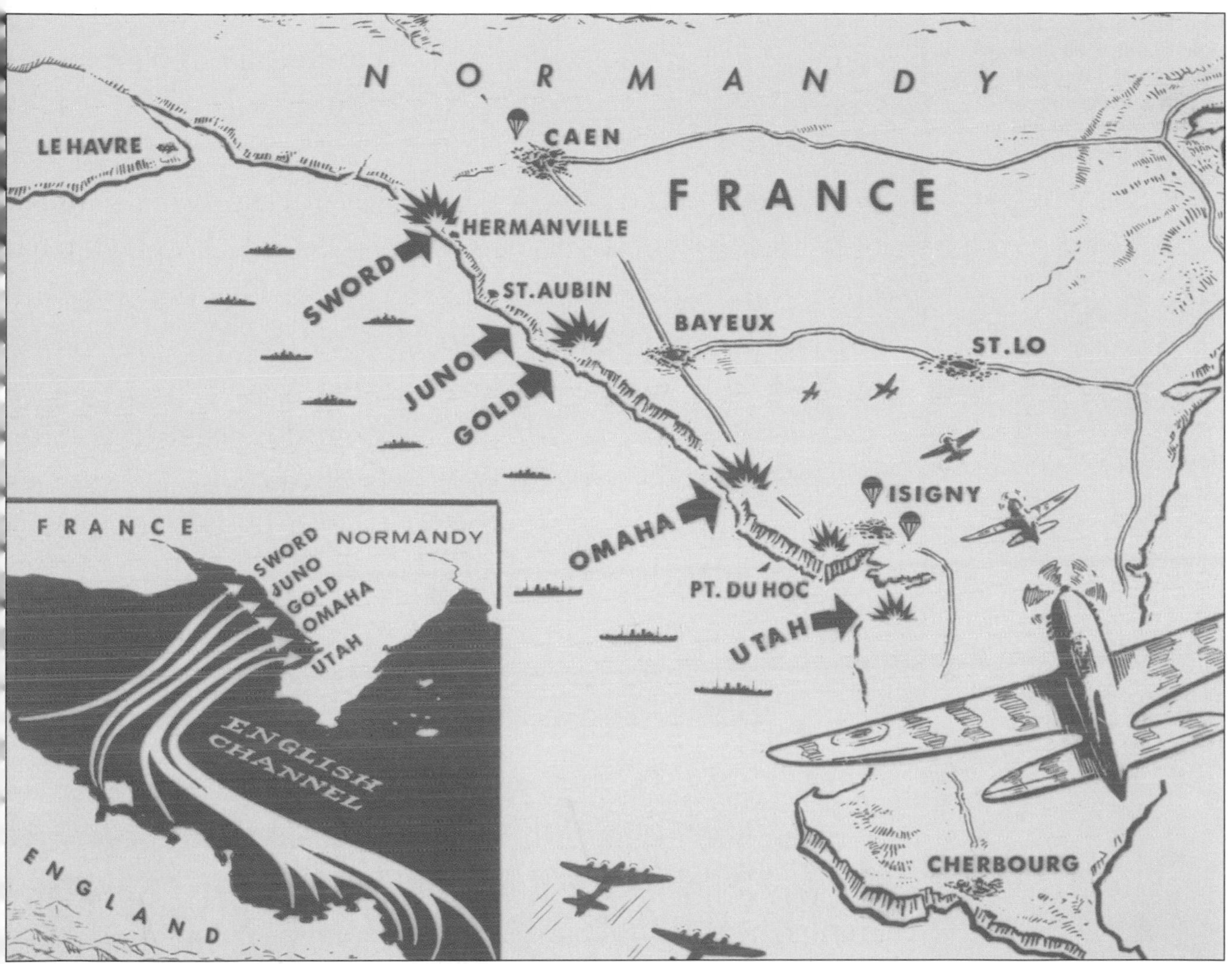

This map shows the locations of the Allied attacks on the coast of France. The names "Sword," "Juno," "Gold," "Omaha," and "Utah" were code names used by the Allied forces.

tanks, trucks, **artillery guns**, **ammunition**, and fuel on the coast of England directly across from Pas de Calais.

Adolf Hitler did not agree. Instead, he thought the Allies would strike in a part of northern France called Normandy. It was farther down the coast from Pas de Calais and much farther across the Channel from the British coast.

From left to right, British Field Marshal Sir Bernard Montgomery, General Dwight Eisenhower, and General Omar Bradley consult a map.

Hitler was right. Allied military leaders U.S. General Dwight Eisenhower and British Field Marshal Sir Bernard Montgomery had decided to invade at Normandy. The German scout planes that had reported the buildup of weapons across from Pas de Calais were unable to get close enough for the pilots to see the truth: The weapons were not real. The guns and vehicles were made out of wood, wire, canvas, and rubber. These fake weapons were made at one of England's film studios, by people skilled at producing such things for movies. The fake weapons were a trick to convince the Germans that the invasion would be at Pas de Calais.

NORMANDY BECOMES A FORTRESS

Field Marshal Erwin Rommel, the German officer in command of the Normandy area, also believed the Allies would invade at Normandy. If they did, he wanted to stop them on the beaches, or in the water. He told his officers, "The enemy must be **annihilated** before he reaches our main battlefield. We must stop him in the water, not only delaying him but destroying all his equipment while it is still afloat."

Field Marshal Erwin Rommel was nicknamed the Desert Fox for his brilliant military direction in Africa during World War II.

Rommel did everything he could to make the 600-mile (960-km) strip of Normandy beaches impossible to break through. He ordered the construction of steel beams joined together at one end, so that they stuck out in various directions. Hundreds of thousands of these were placed along the edge of the shore. At high tide they were underwater and could not be seen. Landing crafts (small boats that carried soldiers to shore) could get caught by the beams and become unable to move. Also, the water along the beaches was filled with mines. Mines are explosive devices that would blow the bottom out of any boat that bumped into them.

Rommel had most of his men in position at the beaches. They were armed mainly with rifles, machine guns, mortars, and rocket launchers. An experienced soldier could fire a rifle about twenty times a minute. Machine guns could fire 1,200 bullets a minute. A mortar was a missile launcher that shot a heavy bomb through the air. When the bomb hit the ground it exploded and could kill or injure anyone close enough. For targets that were farther away, rocket launchers could shoot six explosive **projectiles** at a time.

The Germans also had artillery guns that could fire explosive shells as far as 7 miles (11.3 km). Many such guns were housed in steel-and-concrete structures, known as bunkers, beyond the beach. Thousands of German soldiers

Artillery guns inside bunkers were used to protect the coastline.

Underwater at high tide, these tripods could damage landing crafts heading for the beach.

would use machine guns, mortar bombs, and rockets to direct steady fire at the Allied soldiers trying to get ashore.

Rommel knew the invasion would not come only from the sea. Parachute troops, known as paratroopers, would drop out of the sky. Gliders would come sailing down filled with soldiers. He prepared for these too. Low-lying areas of land behind the beaches were flooded so that paratroopers would come down into water over their heads. Open fields and meadows were filled with rows of trimmed tree trunks set firmly into the ground. Gliders trying to land would be ripped apart. The German soldiers nicknamed these rows of projecting poles "Rommel's asparagus," because they resembled fields of giant asparagus.

THE FRENCH UNDERGROUND

Many French people belonged to what was called the Underground. It was a secret organization that spied on the Germans to help the Allies. Its members provided the Allies with information about German defenses along the Normandy coast. They also caused trouble for German troops, such as damaging equipment and vehicles.

American troops of the 28th Infantry Division march down the Champs Elysees in Paris, France, in 1944.

TANKS, FOOT SOLDIERS, AND SKY SOLDIERS

Each of the armies taking part in the invasion were formed of organizations called divisions. There were infantry divisions (foot soldiers), armored divisions (tanks), and airborne divisions (parachute troops and troops in gliders). An American infantry division was made up of about 16,000 men and

fifty-four artillery guns. A British infantry division had about 18,000 men and seventy-two guns. An American armored division had about 15,000 men, 227 tanks, and fifty-four guns. British and Canadian armored divisions were much the same as American ones.

Germany had been fighting steadily since 1941 and had suffered heavy losses of men and tanks. Their divisions were weaker than those of the Allies. A German infantry division had about 12,000 men and forty-eight guns. An armored division had some 13,000 men and about one hundred tanks or less. In both the Allied and German armies, a number of divisions were grouped together to form an organization called a corps (pronounced "core"). Several corps formed an army.

The Allied commanders planned to invade along a 50-mile (81-km) stretch of Normandy's coastline. They had divided this area into five regions called beaches. Each beach was

"Utah" was the code name for this area of the coast, located on the eastern shore of the Cotentin Peninsula.

given a special name. From west to east these were Utah, Omaha, Gold, Juno, and Sword. Each beach was to be attacked separately.

THE BEACHES OF NORMANDY

The area called Utah Beach is on the east side of a **peninsula** that sticks out of the French coastline. It is a narrow area of sand dotted with dunes and flat, marshy land. A long concrete seawall—a high wall to keep water from getting too far onto the beach at high tide—ran along the far edge of the beach where the marsh begins. The Germans had flooded the marshland to make the invasion more difficult. The only way through the marshland was by five raised roads. Allied soldiers would try to gain control of the roads and move up the coast to capture the port city of Cherbourg. Cherbourg could then be used to bring in supplies and ammunition.

Omaha Beach, to the east of Utah, is a very different sort of place. It is a curving stretch of sand that slopes up to a line of rugged cliffs. A concrete seawall ran along the bottom of the cliffs. Machine guns, rocket launchers, and mortars were hidden along the slopes and crests of the cliffs beyond the seawall. Farther back, on the flat land stretching away from the cliff tops, were artillery guns of all sizes. Omaha Beach was to be the target of the 1st and 29th infantry divisions of the U.S. V Corps.

Cherbourg, France, was a major target during the D-Day attack. The Allies wanted to gain control of this important port city.

The high cliffs at Pointe du Hoc would make the attack on Omaha Beach especially difficult.

* * * *

At the western end of Omaha is Pointe du Hoc. High cliffs look down on this narrow stretch of beach. On top of the cliffs were five big guns that could fire onto any part of Utah or Omaha. Pointe du Hoc would be the special target of several companies of highly trained troops. Their mission was to destroy the guns.

Gold, Juno, and Sword were areas on a long stretch of beach from the east end of Omaha Beach to where the Orne River flows into the English Channel. There are a number of little towns along the beach. The Germans had **fortified** most of them, putting mines, barbed wire, and **barricades** in the streets, and soldiers and guns in many of the houses. The areas of beach around and between the towns were filled with thousands of hidden mines. All along the edges of these beaches were obstacles to prevent boats from getting through. The object of the Canadian and British forces invading these beaches was to push forward and capture the cities of Bayeux and Caen. This would give the Allies a route to Paris, the German army's headquarters in France.

TIME, TIDE, AND WEATHER

The Allied commanders carefully planned every part of the invasion. They decided to invade all the beaches at low tide. When the tide is low, water does not reach up very far onto a beach. Most of the obstacles the Germans had put in the water along the beaches would be clearly visible and could be avoided. The invasion would take place in June, and the tide would be at its lowest on June 4, 5, and 6. The supreme Allied commander, General Eisenhower, selected

June 5 as the day of the invasion. That day became known as D-Day. The whole plan for the invasion was called Operation Overlord.

General Eisenhower (center) originally selected June 5 as the day of the invasion. He is shown here seated with Field Marshal Montgomery (left) and General Bradley.

The commanders knew that the Germans would be expecting them to invade at night, under cover of darkness. So they decided to make the invasion at 6:30 in the morning, when it would be light. This might take the Germans by surprise. Six-thirty on the morning of June 5 became known as H-Hour.

June arrived with stormy weather, and the storms continued each day. The Channel was swept by fierce winds that caused high waves. Many of the smaller ships of the invasion fleet could not cross the Channel in such weather. On June 3, General Eisenhower pushed the invasion back to June 6. He hoped for better weather.

For the invasion to take place at 6:30 A.M. on June 6, all the ships would have to be in the Channel by noon on June 5. Army **meteorologists** told General Eisenhower that the weather might clear up by the afternoon of June 5. But if Eisenhower ordered the invasion to begin and the stormy weather continued, the ships would have to be called back at the last moment. That would ruin everything. If the invasion had to be called off, it would be a whole month before the tide on the Normandy coast would be low enough again. During that time, the Germans would surely find out about the plan. General Eisenhower had to make a difficult decision. At 4:15 on the morning of June 5 he told his commanders, "Okay, we'll go."

General Eisenhower gives a last minute pep-talk to paratroopers before the start of the invasion.

On the horizon, a seemingly endless stream of ships can be seen making their way across the Channel.

BAD WEATHER HELPS THE ALLIES

By noon on June 5, about 5,000 ships from the invasion fleet were out in the Channel. It was the biggest invasion fleet in the history of the world. Transport and landing ships carried men, tanks, and other vehicles. There were also more than seven hundred warships from the United States, Britain, Canada, and France.

The USS *New Jersey* was one of several new battleships used during World War II.

The weather was still quite bad. A fierce wind whipped the water. The ships rolled and pitched in the strong waves. Most of the soldiers were seasick, throwing up into paper bags. When those became useless, men threw up into their helmets.

But the stormy weather became an advantage for the Allies. Because of the bad weather, the German Navy canceled its patrols into the English Channel, and the German

Air Force called off its scouting flights over the Channel. If just one German ship or plane had seen the invasion fleet coming, the Germans would have had hours to prepare.

In addition, German commanders were sure the Allies could never invade in such terrible weather. In fact, Field Marshal Rommel had gone to Germany for a short vacation, and most of the other generals were away at a special meeting. At the very moment the invasion would begin, most of the top commanders in Normandy would be miles away.

This photograph shows a navigator inside the cockpit of a German plane in 1944.

Allied forces attacked the city of Caen.

ATTACK FROM THE SKY!

By 11:30 P.M. on June 5, the first of the aircraft that had taken off from Britain were arriving over the Normandy coast. German commanders began to get reports of large groups of heavy bombers. Crews of **anti-aircraft guns** ran to the pits and aimed their guns toward the sky. Soldiers guarding the beaches saw flickering lights and heard explosions from the direction of the distant city of Caen, where bombs were falling. The bombers were destroying the main roads through Caen so that the Germans could not use them for moving troops to the beaches.

SECRET MESSAGES

On the night of June 5, British radio announcers began saying strange things on radio programs heard in France. For example, they said things like "It is hot in Suez." These were actually coded messages to the French Underground about how to help the invasion. "It is hot in Suez" was a way of telling members of the Underground to begin damaging railroad tracks so that the Germans would be unable to move troops quickly by train.

Heavily armed American paratroopers sit inside a military plane on their way to the Normandy coast.

At about 2:00 A.M., thousands of white circles began appearing in the dark sky beyond the beaches. Troops of the U.S. 82nd and 101st Airborne Divisions and British 6th Airborne Division were coming down into the French countryside by parachute. In other places, British troops were sailing down in gliders. Eighteen thousand Allied soldiers were dropping out of the sky. The first part of the invasion had begun.

This attack from the sky was not a complete success. Many paratroopers came down in the wrong places. Some were captured. Others were shot before they even reached the ground.

* * * *

Some came down in flooded places and were drowned. A number of the British gliders smashed into Rommel's asparagus, killing or injuring the soldiers inside.

Still, many of the airborne soldiers were able to carry out their missions. They blew up bridges so that German tanks would not be able to get across rivers. They cut telephone lines so German commanders could not give orders to their troops. They wiped out groups of German soldiers guarding crossroads and took control of the roads themselves. A force of paratroopers captured the town of Sainte-Mere-Eglise from the German troops holding it. This would prevent the Germans from moving any troops on the railroad that ran through the town.

INVASION OR DIVERSION?

Reports of all this started coming into German army headquarters from all over Normandy. Many officers urged that troops and tanks be sent quickly to **reinforce** the German forces there, but Field Marshal von Rundstedt refused. He believed this was all a diversion, a trick to draw attention away from Pas de Calais. He still believed the real invasion would come there.

German radar units along the coast began to pick up frightening signals from the English Channel. Their radar screens showed thousands of blips—white spots on the dark screen—indicating objects coming across the Channel toward Normandy. Most of the men who had been left in command in Normandy felt sure this was a mistake.

As radar screens indicated approaching ships, German military officers kept a close watch on the English Channel.

Worried German officers along the coast, however, began staring at the Channel through binoculars. At first they saw nothing but water with a faint mist hanging over it. Then, suddenly, dark shapes came sliding out of the mist. Shocked, the Germans swung their binoculars to peer from one side to another. As far as they could see in either direction, thousands of ships were coming toward them. It was definitely the invasion!

Phones began to ring at those headquarters that had not had their phone lines cut. Officers who answered them heard reports of thousands of ships approaching. Many refused to believe such a thing.

UTAH BEACH

Allied bombers attacked Utah Beach. Bunkers were destroyed, and machine-gun nests and gun positions were wiped out. Then warships began firing onto the beach. Shell bursts tore barbed wire apart and exploded the mines buried in the sand. The German soldiers defending the beach huddled helplessly in their hiding places. The time reached 6:30. H-Hour!

As troops head for the beach, naval gunfire had already begun in an attempt to break down German resistance.

Soldiers wade through water and dodge bullets as they struggle to reach land.

LANDING CRAFTS

A landing craft, or LC, was a small boat that held thirty-six soldiers. LCs were carried on a large ship and lowered into the water near shore. The boats were steered into shallow water at the beach by sailors.

At the far end of Utah Beach, confused Germans were surprised to see tanks coming up out of the water. These were tanks known as DDs, an Allied secret weapon. They could move through water, kept afloat by huge water wings made of canvas. At least a dozen DDs came onto the beach with their guns spitting. Behind them came the soldiers of the U.S. 4th Division. Most of them still gagging from seasickness, they struggled through the water and onto the beach. They were met by only a few scattered rifle shots.

In truth, the American landing at this part of Utah Beach was a mistake. The boats guiding the landing crafts had gone off course. The landing crafts were coming in almost one mile (1.6 km) from where they were supposed to. But this was another piece of good luck for the Allies. This area of Utah Beach was defended by a second-rate German division. As the Americans reached their positions, most of the enemy soldiers surrendered; others ran away. By 9:00 A.M., Utah Beach was completely in American hands.

Soldiers advance over the top of a concrete seawall after a successful landing on Utah Beach.

POINTE DU HOC

At Pointe du Hoc, a few miles east of Utah Beach, there was silence at H-Hour. Four DUKWs—boats with wheels that could move on land—and landing crafts carrying special troops called Rangers reached the Normandy beach at H-Hour. They discovered that they were 3 miles (4.8 km) away from Pointe du Hoc, so they turned and headed back along the shore. German troops quickly fired on them.

Reaching their target at 7:10, the men of the two Ranger battalions rushed ashore, heading for the cliffs. At the cliffs they shot grappling hooks attached to rope ladders up to the top. Some hooks failed to catch and fell back down. Others caught on rocks and in the barbed wire that was strung

All aspects of the invasion were carefully planned. Here, soldiers use amphibious landing crafts, which operate both in the sea and on land, to rehearse the actual events of D-Day.

This photograph shows a German machine gun nest captured by Canadian troops.

along the clifftops. Rangers began to swarm up the ladders while German soldiers threw grenades down at them.

British and American destroyers moved in close to shore. They now opened fire, raining shells down onto the top of the cliff. The Germans were forced to run back to their bunkers, and the Rangers began squirming over the edge of the cliff. They found the concrete bunkers shattered. The German soldiers had all run away.

The Rangers went looking for the guns they had come to destroy and soon found them, abandoned. The Rangers exploded grenades inside the barrels, making the guns unable to fire. Of the 225 Rangers who were sent to Pointe du Hoc, only ninety were left, but the mission had been accomplished. There, too, the invasion was a success.

Special tanks were used to carry out the invasion. As the troops moved farther inland, they used tanks like these to plow through trees and shrubs.

GOLD BEACH

At Gold Beach, underwater obstacles caused trouble for the British 50th Division. Some landing crafts were blown up, and others were snagged and torn open. It took almost an hour before any boats reached the beach.

The British had planned to send tanks onto the beach before any men. Besides DD tanks, they had tanks to do special things. Petard tanks had special cannons for destroying concrete bunkers. Tanks called crocodiles shot jets of fire. "Crabs" were tanks that pounded the ground with chains to explode mines and make a clear path for foot soldiers. The British soldiers called all these special tanks "funnies."

★ ★ ★ ★

The DD tanks could not swim through all the obstacles, however. They could not be sent in until the boats carrying them could get close to shore. Foot soldiers, still half seasick, were first onto the beach. They quickly found that the bombs dropped by the airplanes and the shells fired by ships had missed their targets. The villages were undamaged and the beach was thick with mines.

Soon after, crab tanks moved slowly forward, making paths through the mines. Petard tanks blasted bunkers open. Crocodiles spouted flames into houses where German soldiers and weapons were hidden. British foot soldiers followed, firing machine guns and throwing grenades. Within an hour, they had wiped out most of the resistance. Gold Beach was taken.

A mortar crew prepares to fire into German positions along the coast.

After a successful landing, British troops fought their way into nearby French towns to recapture them from the Germans.

JUNO AND SWORD BEACHES

At Juno Beach, rough seas, sharp rocks, and underwater obstacles also held up the landings. Twenty of the first twenty-four landing crafts were sunk or damaged. Thirty-four of forty tanks never reached the beach.

Canadian and British troops dashed ashore under heavy fire. They fought their way past bunkers and trenches into the towns. They fought from street to street, and many soldiers were killed. But behind them, more and more troops and tanks were pouring onto the beach and moving forward. Juno Beach was in Allied hands.

At Sword Beach, five crab tanks were ashore first. They moved slowly forward, their chains fiercely slamming the sand. Reaching the road, they stopped and began firing their guns at the German bunkers and trenches.

* * * *

Behind them came thirty-one DD tanks. They, too, moved forward, firing. Next were six hundred infantry. They spread out, heading for the towns, where they began fighting from street to street.

By 9:00, all German troops had pulled back or surrendered. Sword Beach was conquered. Juno and Sword were now under Allied control.

TROUBLE AT OMAHA BEACH

At Omaha Beach things went wrong from the start. Of the thirty-two DD tanks launched at H-Hour, twenty-seven sank straight to the bottom due to rough waters. Many landing crafts filled with water, and ten sank before ever reaching the shore. Many men drowned.

Landing crafts head for Omaha Beach.

ARTIFICIAL HARBORS

A harbor is a sheltered place where ships can anchor and unload their cargoes. The Allies created two artificial harbors for the invasion. These were built in sections that were towed to Omaha and Gold beaches and put together. They were very useful in helping the Allies bring ammunition and supplies to keep the invasion going.

Allied bombers should have destroyed the guns defending the beach, but they had missed their targets. Many of the landing crafts that had not sunk were being blown apart by German gunfire. Men in them were hurled into the sea. Some of those who survived were pulled out of the water by men in other boats.

Despite all this, landing crafts kept on coming. Many of the boats failed to get close enough to shore. When men rushed out of them they found themselves in water up to their necks or even over their heads. They struggled to swim, but soldiers with radio equipment or other heavy objects strapped to their backs had no chance. They went straight to the bottom like stones and drowned.

Members of an American landing party help their fellow soldiers safely onto shore.

Injured soldiers on Omaha Beach wait for medical help.

The men who reached the beach were under heavy fire. The edge of the beach was dotted with motionless bodies. The surviving men simply could not move any farther. Some hid behind steel-girder tank obstacles while others tried to dig themselves into the sand or crouched in the water. The invasion of Omaha Beach was being stopped cold.

A victory at Omaha Beach was necessary for the invasion to succeed.

"BLOODY" OMAHA

Three hours after the start of H-Hour, four of the five Normandy beaches were in Allied hands, but Omaha Beach had still not been captured. It was a scene of horror. More than two thousand dead and wounded men lay on the yellow sand. The air was dark with the smoke of burning American tanks. Men were still coming in on landing crafts, but they simply sought shelter. No one was moving forward. Allied commanders began to fear that the invasion at Omaha Beach was a failure.

If the German army had made a **counterattack** at this time, the invasion could have been defeated. German forces could easily have wiped out the Americans on Omaha Beach. The Germans could then have attacked the Allied troops on Utah and Gold beaches from the side. This would have meant almost certain victory for the Germans. Everything could have turned in Germany's favor. Germany might even have won the war.

★ ★ ★ ★

But most German leaders still believed the Normandy invasion was just a trick. They still expected the real invasion to come somewhere else. So they held their tanks and troops back, keeping them ready.

Suddenly, from their hiding places, the Allied soldiers saw a man walking around as if he had no fear of bullets or explosions. It was Brigadier General Norman Cota, assistant commander of the 29th Division. Cota walked to the seawall and began giving the men directions. He ordered a section of seawall blown out with an explosive charge so that the soldiers could get up onto the cliffs to attack the German troops. By the hundreds, men left their hiding places and ran to the seawall. They began moving up to the high ground. They blasted bunkers with hand grenades and shot or captured German soldiers in trenches.

EISENHOWER PREPARES TO TAKE THE BLAME

When General Eisenhower heard what was happening at Omaha Beach, he began to think the invasion might fail. In case this happened, he wrote a short message to read over the radio to the people of the United States and Great Britain. It ended with the words "If any blame or fault attaches to the attempt, it is mine alone."

German prisoners of war are led away by Allied forces.

American destroyers moved in close to shore and began firing at the German positions farther back from the beach. At 1:30 P.M., General Omar Bradley received a message that American soldiers were in full possession of the beach and were moving inland. Now on Omaha Beach, too, the invasion had succeeded!

The Allies were now able to complete their buildup. Men, guns, tanks, and supplies were brought onto the beaches. Landing crafts brought in trucks filled with ammunition for artillery guns and gasoline for tanks. The trucks belonged to what were called Quartermaster Truck Regiments, and the drivers were all African-Americans. They were in just as much danger as the foot soldiers. They had to drive through minefields and shell bursts that were exploding on the roads. A number of drivers were awarded Bronze Star and Silver Star medals for their courage in getting ammunition, fuel, supplies, and soldiers to where they were needed.

THE NORMANDY AMERICAN CEMETERY

Overlooking Omaha Beach is an area of land that was given to the United States by the French government. More than 9,000 headstones of polished white marble crosses and Stars of David stand above the beach. Beneath them lie the remains of Americans who were killed on D-Day and in other battles in Normandy in the weeks afterward.

After capturing Omaha Beach, American troops stand by as men, guns, tanks, and supplies arrive.

THE DAY THAT SAVED FREEDOM

D-Day was a turning point of World War II, signaling the end of the Nazi regime. Here, U.S. troops hold a captured Nazi flag in France.

By the end of the day, 176,000 Allied soldiers were moving deeper into France, with thousands more behind them. The invasion was a success. The armies of Nazi Germany were in retreat. There were still months of fighting ahead, but D-Day was the beginning of the end for Nazi Germany.

D-Day was one of the most important events of the twentieth century. It was the battle that showed that the Allies would win the war. For France, Belgium, the Netherlands, and other nations occupied by German forces, D-Day was the beginning of hope for freedom. For the people of the United States, Great Britain, and Canada, it meant their freedom was secure. Adolf Hitler and his dream of ruling the world were fading away. Ten months after D-Day, Hitler killed himself. Germany soon surrendered.

The exact number of men who were killed on D-Day is not known for sure. It is believed that at least five thousand Allied soldiers died that day. Those men gave their lives so that our freedom and our way of life would continue.

Glossary

ally (*plural* allies)—a friendly nation; nations working together for a common purpose

ammunition—objects that are fired from a gun

annihilated—completely wiped out

anti-aircraft guns—cannons or machine guns that can fire projectiles high enough into the sky to destroy enemy aircraft

artificial—made by man, not by nature

artillery guns—heavy guns able to fire long distances

barricades—roadblocks set up to stop people from getting through

counterattack—an attack made against an enemy force that is attacking

dictator—a person who holds absolute power

fortified—strengthened

glider—an aircraft without an engine

meteorologist—a person who studies Earth's atmosphere to predict the weather

peninsula—a piece of land that projects out from a coastline

projectiles—missiles that are shot from a weapon

reinforce—to bring more troops to add to the strength of troops facing a battle

Timeline: D-Day

1943

MAY 12–27
The date for the invasion of northwest Europe is tentatively set as May 1, 1944.

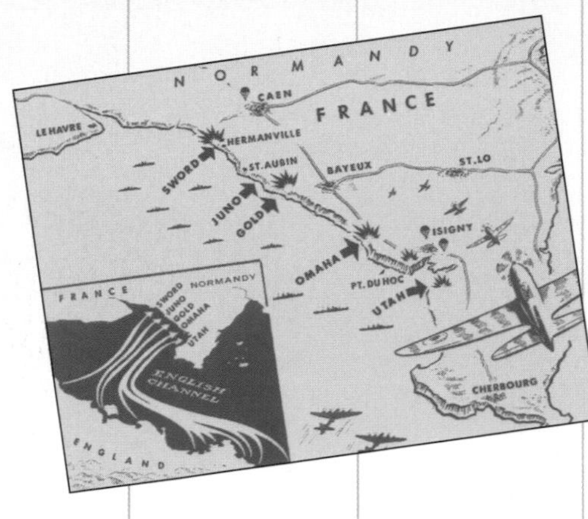

JULY 15
A team of American and British officers are given responsibility for planning the invasion, known as Operation Overlord. They issue a report stating that the invasion will be the largest, most complicated military operation in history.

DECEMBER 24
U.S. General Dwight Eisenhower is named commander of Operation Overlord.

1944

JANUARY 23
The plan for the invasion of Normandy is approved by Allied military leaders.

JANUARY 31
Allied military leaders settle on early June for the invasion.

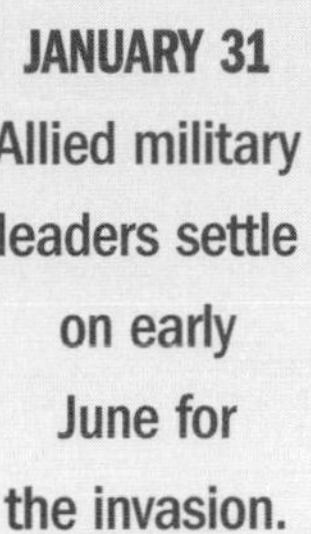

MAY 16
General Eisenhower picks June 5 as D-Day—the day of the invasion.

JUNE 3
General Eisenhower postpones D-Day from June 5 to June 6, hoping for better weather.

JUNE 5
General Eisenhower gives the final order to go ahead. The invasion fleet leaves England by noon. Bombers and aircraft carrying airborne troops begin taking off as soon as darkness falls.

JUNE 6
Allied forces begin landing on the coast of Normandy at 6:30 A.M. By nightfall, 176,000 Allied troops are in France.

To Find Out More

BOOKS

Amis, Nancy. *The Orphans of Normandy*. New York: Atheneum, 2003.

Schultz, Randy. *Dwight D. Eisenhower*. Springfield, NJ: Enslow Publishers, 2003.

Shuter, Jane. *Life and Death in Hitler's Europe*. Portsmouth, NH: Heinemann, 2003.

ONLINE SITES

World War II, Britannica Online
http://search.eb.com/normandy/studyguide/index.html

D-Day, American Experience
http://www.pbs.org/wgbh/amex/dday

Eyewitness Memories of WWII
http://www.normandy1944.info/

Index

Bold numbers indicate illustrations.

African-Americans, 40
Allied attacks on French coast, map, 7
Artificial harbors, 35
Artillery guns, 10, **10**

Beaches of Normandy, 13–15, **14**, **16**, 17
Bradley, Omar, **8**, **18**, 40
Bunkers, 10, **10**

Caen, France, 23, **23**
Cota, Norman, 39

DD tanks, 28, 33, 43
DUKWs, 30, **30**

Eisenhower, Dwight, 8, **8**, 17–19, **18**, **19**, 39
English Channel, 20

France, 4, 5–8. *See also* Normandy
French Underground, 11, 23

Germany, 4, 9–11, 13, 25
Gold Beach, 17, 32–33
Great Britain, 4, 5–8, 13, 17, 24, 34

H-Hour, 18, 27, 30
Hitler, Adolf, 4, **4**, 7, 8, 41

Japan, 5
Juno Beach, 17, 34–35

Landing crafts, 28, **28**, **35**

Military divisions
  Airborne/paratroopers, **24**, 24–25
  armored, 13
  (*See also* tanks)
  infantry/foot soldiers, 12–13
  Rangers, 30–31
Montgomery, Bernard, 8, **8**, **18**

Navigator inside German plane, **22**
Nazis, 4
Normandy, 9–11, 13–15, **14**, **16**, 17, 27–40
Normandy American Cemetery, 40

Omaha Beach, 15, 35–40, **38**, **40**
Operation Overlord, 18

Pas de Calais, France, 6–8, 25
Pearl Harbor, 5
Pointe du Hoc, **16**, 17, 30–31

Radio programs, 23
Rommel, Erwin, **9**, 9–11, 22
Rundstedt, Gerd von, 6, 25

Sainte-Mere-Eglise, France, 25
Secret messages, 23
Soldiers/troops
  British, **34**
  German cavalry, **5**
  German prisoners, **39**
  landing party, **36**
  mortar crew, **33**
  U.S. Army, 10th Mountain Division, **6**
  U.S. 28th Infantry Division, **12–13**
Sword Beach, 17, 34–35

Tanks, 28, **32**, 32–33, 34–35

USS *New Jersey*, **21**
Utah Beach, 14, **14**, 27–29, **29**

About the Author

Tom McGowen is a children's book author with a special interest in military history, on which he has written seventeen previous books. His most recent book in the Cornerstones of Freedom Series was *The Surrender at Appomattox*. As an author of more than sixty books for young readers, fiction and nonfiction, he has received the Children's Reading Round Table Annual Award for Outstanding Contributions to the Field of Children's Literature.